A THOUSAND CRANES

by

Kathryn Schultz Miller

Dramatic Publishing
Woodstock, Illinois • England • Australia • New Zealand

A THOUSAND CRANES

A Play in One Act
For One Male and Two Females with doubling

CHARACTERS

SADAKO .... a twelve-year-old Japanese girl
living in Hiroshima
KENJI .... Sadako's fourteen-year-old friend
(also plays ACTOR 1 and FATHER)
GRANDMOTHER OBA CHAN .... the spirit of
Sadako's deceased Grandmother
(also plays ACTOR 2 and MOTHER)

TIME: 1955

PLACE: Hiroshima, Japan

Special thanks to my husband, Barry Miller,
and my good friends and associates
Dain Paige and Dahn Schwarz
for their contributions to this work.

A THOUSAND CRANES

AT RISE: *The playing area is a circle of about 20 feet by 20 feet. Audience is seated on three sides of the playing area. Upstage R of the circle will be a musical or instrument "station" with percussion instruments and recorded music arranged in such a way that at appropriate times actors may sit comfortably on a stool and contribute music and sound effects to the performance. UL are standing fans of various pastels and varying heights, the tallest being less than 5 feet. To the left and right downstage are two white masks on each side in tube holders about waist high. GRANDMOTHER OBA CHAN will wear a magnificent Japanese mask. ACTORS 1 and 2 will carry white masks when playing the parts of the DOCTORS. SPIRITS will be indicated by red masks on holders but will not actually be worn by actors. SADAKO, KENJI, MOTHER and FATHER, will not wear masks. ACTORS 1 and 2 will wear all black. SADAKO wears a simple western-style school uniform of a skirt and blouse with a tie.*

The play begins in silence. ACTORS 1 and 2 bow to each other before the music stand. SADAKO watches from behind the music stand. ACTORS 1 and 2 mime lifting a large piece of paper off the floor. In mirrored motions, they carry the paper to DC, carefully place it on the floor and gently smooth it out. They bow again, then

5

turn U. SADAKO crosses down to paper as recorded folding music begins. The mood of the music gentle and pleasant. ACTORS 1 and 2 count with SADAKO as she mimes the folding of a larger-than-life crane.

ALL *(punctuating their words with percussion sounds).* One, two, three, four, five, six, seven, eight, nine... *(SADAKO mimes the lifting of the giant bird with both hands. It is very light. She thrusts the bird into flight.)*

SADAKO. Ten. *(SADAKO blows as if to launch it. ALL watch it in the sky, from left to right. To AUDIENCE.)* My name is Sadako. I was born in Japan in 1943. My home was called Hiroshima. *(Quiet sound effects come from ACTORS 1 and 2.)* When I was two years old, my mother held me in her arms. She sang a song to me. *(ACTOR 2 sings a soothing, quiet melody.)* It was a quiet summer morning. Inside our small house my Grandmother was preparing tea. *(SADAKO pauses while ACTOR 2 sings.)* Suddenly there was a tremendous flash of light that cut across the sky! *(A very, very loud startling BOOM noise. SADAKO falls into a kneeling position, covering her head. When all is quiet she stands.)* My name is Sadako. This is my story. *(A dramatic rhythm beat, not as loud as before and slowly fading.)*

ACTOR 2 *(quietly fading away).* Sixty-seven, sixty-eight, sixty-nine, seventy...

(SADAKO and ACTOR 1, now KENJI, have moved U and now KENJI comes bounding on to playing area, out of breath and laughing. He wears a black cap to distinguish himself as KENJI. He begins to count, determining by how many seconds he has won the race with

SADAKO. As ACTOR 2's counting fades he picks it up. They say the primary numbers, one and two and three, etc., together.)

ACTOR 2 *(fading).* Seventy...seventy-one...seventy-two...
KENJI. One...two...three...four

(SADAKO runs in out of breath and laughing.)

KENJI. Beat you by four seconds!
SADAKO. Four? You're lying!
KENJI *(laughing).* It was actually four and a half, but I let you have that.
SADAKO. Oh! You...! *(Slumping.)* You always win! You should let somebody else win sometime.
KENJI. Why, Sadako. You can't mean that I should cheat so that you can win.
SADAKO. Oh, it wouldn't be cheating so much as...polite.
KENJI *(laughing).* And I suppose when you run in the girl's contest next month you'll want the judges to be *polite* and let somebody else win.
SADAKO. Well, no.
KENJI. I thought so.
SADAKO. Oh, Kenji, do you think I have a chance to win?
KENJI *(mocking).* You? You win a race against the fastest girls in Hiroshima? You can't win.
SADAKO. Why not?
KENJI. Because you're a turtle that's why. A great big lumbering turtle. *(Mimes slow turtle, laughing at his jest.)*
SADAKO. I am not a turtle!

KENJI. Yes, you are.

SADAKO. Am not.

KENJI. Are too.

SADAKO. Well, if I'm a turtle, then you're a frog!

KENJI. A frog?

SADAKO. Yes. A great big green one with warts all over it.

KENJI. Sadako, you can't possibly mean...croak...*(Putting her on.)* Well, where on earth could that have come from? Croak! — Sudden / underhand.

SADAKO. Oh, you.

KENJI. Look, Sadako, my hand is turning green...croak ...and it has warts all over it! *(He crouches to a frog position and sticks out his tongue, leaping around, croaking. Uses bill of his cap to indicate the mouth of the croaking frog.)* Croak! Croak!

SADAKO *(laughing in spite of herself)*. Now, you stop that. *(She is laughing almost uncontrollably, soon KENJI stops and laughs with her. They stop, leaning on each other, gaining composure.)* Kenji, tell me the truth. Do you think I have *any* chance of winning the races next month?

KENJI. Sadako, I will tell you the truth. I believe you will win.

SADAKO *(thrilled)*. You really think so? You really, really do?

KENJI. Yes. I really, really do.

SADAKO. Oh, Kenji! *(She hugs him.)* Wait until I tell my father. He will be so proud of me! *(She starts to go.)*

KENJI. Now don't quit practicing!

SADAKO. Oh, I won't.

KENJI. See you tomorrow?

SADAKO. Tomorrow! *(She moves U as if to exit.)*

(KENJI, now ACTOR 1, moves to instrument station and makes music for scene change. SADAKO moves U as ACTOR 2, now MOTHER, moves into the scene. She is counting out candles and putting them on the table. She wears a kimono. ACTOR 1 counts and then fades as MOTHER joins in and finally ends the counting.)

ACTOR 1. One hundred and eighteen, one hundred and nineteen, one hundred and twenty, one hundred and twenty-one, one hundred and twenty-two...one hundred and twenty-three...*(Again, they speak the primary numbers together.)*

MOTHER *(counting candles)*. One...two...three...four...

(SADAKO comes running in, very excited.)

SADAKO. Mother, Mother! Wait till you hear! I have wonderful news!

MOTHER *(not looking up, continues working)*. Your shoes, Sadako.

SADAKO. Oh. *(She calms down to remove her shoes, puts them by the door, then rushes back to MOTHER.)* Wait till I tell you!

MOTHER. Sadako, show your respect to your elders.

SADAKO. Oh. *(She bows, puts hands together as in prayer and bows her head toward MOTHER.)* Mother, Kenji just told me...!

MOTHER. Sadako, show your respect to our beloved ancestors. *(Disheartened, SADAKO kneels before an imaginary shrine, hands in prayer and bowing her head. Returns to MOTHER, somewhat subdued.)*

SADAKO. Mother, I...

MOTHER. You must wait for your father to tell this earth-shattering news. Now it is time to prepare for dinner.

SADAKO. But, Mother...

MOTHER. Sushi has been prepared, the rice plates have been set. Sadako, you may warm the saki for your father.

SADAKO. Yes, Mother. *(MOTHER straightens candles on the table.)*

(FATHER enters, takes off his shoes.)

SADAKO. Father! *(She runs to him, grabs him in embrace and almost twirls him around.)* Wait till I tell you!

FATHER. Well, what is this?

MOTHER *(not angry)*. This daughter of yours will not learn discipline.

FATHER. Your mother is right, Sadako. You must learn moderation in all things.

SADAKO. But, Father, I have such wonderful news!

FATHER *(warm)*. It seems that everything in your world is wonderful, Sadako. *(Kisses the top of her head.)* You may tell us your news.

SADAKO *(looks anxiously at them BOTH)*. Now?

FATHER *(laughing)*. Now, Sadako.

SADAKO. Kenji says I'm fast enough to win the race next month! Isn't that wonderful? He thinks I can *win!*

FATHER *(genuinely impressed)*. You have been practicing very hard.

SADAKO. Oh, yes, Father. Kenji and I run every day.

FATHER. Kenji is a fast runner, an excellent athlete.

SADAKO. Yes, he is, Father. And a good teacher, too.

MOTHER. Even so, you must use discipline to practice very hard if you really want to win.

SADAKO. Oh, I want to win, Mother. I want to win more than anything on earth!

FATHER. We are very proud of you, Sadako. *(BOTH parents hug her. MOTHER begins to light candles.)*

SADAKO. Mother, why are you lighting candles on the table?

MOTHER. Soon it will be Oban, Sadako.

FATHER. It is the day of the spirits.

MOTHER. We light a candle for our ancestors who have died.

FATHER. We ask them to return to us and join in our celebration of life.

MOTHER *(has lit all but last candle)*. This one is for Oba chan, your Grandmother.

SADAKO. I remember her. I was only a baby, but I remember how warm my grandmother's hands were. *(She kneels before the candles. MOTHER and FATHER move away. Their lines now sound like statements in a dream.)*

FATHER. Oba chan died in the Thunderbolt.

SADAKO. She had a gentle voice.

MOTHER. Suddenly there was a great flash of light.

SADAKO. Her smile was like sunshine.

FATHER. It cut through the sky!

SADAKO. Grandmother? Grandmother?

MOTHER. The world was filled with blinding light. *(MOTHER and FATHER spin away with arms up in protecting gesture. They twirl to their places behind the music stand where they make percussion sounds.)*

SADAKO. Can you hear me, Grandmother?

FATHER. It took our friends.

SADAKO. Can your spirit really return like they say?

MOTHER. It took our home.

SADAKO. Are you watching me now? Do you see me when I run?

FATHER. It took your Grandmother, Oba chan.

(MOTHER and FATHER now become ACTOR 1 and ACTOR 2. They use a percussion sound that builds and when it stops the silence is startling. They begin to count.)

ACTORS 1 and 2. One hundred and fifty-one...

SADAKO. One. *(Blows out first candle.)*

ACTORS 1 and 2. One hundred and fifty-two...

SADAKO. Two. *(Blows out second candle.)*

ACTORS 1 and 2. One hundred and fifty-three...

SADAKO. Three. *(Blows out third candle.)*

ACTORS 1 and 2. One hundred and fifty-four...

SADAKO *(before the candle of her GRANDMOTHER, looks up)*. Will I win my race, Grandmother? Can you hear me now? *(Turns back to candle.)* Four. *(Blows out candle, stands and looks around.)* Grandmother?

(ACTOR 1 plays a loud dramatic percussion sound that fades. ACTOR 2, using the voice she will use later as GRANDMOTHER speaks.)

ACTOR 2/GRANDMOTHER *(as she moves slowly, twirling away until she is hidden behind the largest fan)*. I hear you, Sadako!

(The loud cymbal sound comes again and fades into a new sound. Now a fast, quick staccato sound is heard from the instrument stand. ACTOR 1 also is KENJI,

using only the voice from his location. ACTOR 2 turns U to put on GRANDMOTHER OBA CHAN's mask. SADAKO begins to run in place.)

KENJI *(moving D to replace set piece and back to music stand.)* You little turtle, you'll never win at that speed. *(SADAKO speaks as if he is beside her, running.)*

SADAKO *(running)*. I am not a turtle!

KENJI. Sure you are, that's how fast turtles run, isn't it?

SADAKO. Croak, croak, croak! *(They BOTH laugh.)*

KENJI. I bet I can make it to the river before you!

SADAKO. Bet you can't.

KENJI. Bet I can!

SADAKO. Bet you can't. *(She runs faster in place as percussion sound also speeds up.)*

(ACTOR 2, who now becomes GRANDMOTHER OBA CHAN, turns and raises her arms. Her costume and mask are magnificent. A majestic sound is used by ACTOR 1 to accompany her movement. SADAKO is becoming out of breath. GRANDMOTHER makes a magical gesture toward SADAKO. SADAKO trips and falls.)

KENJI *(still out of scene)*. Sadako, are you all right?

SADAKO *(rubbing her hip)*. Oooh...

KENJI. Here, let me help you up. *(She takes his imaginary hand and stands.)* Are you all right?

SADAKO. Yes, I'm fine.

KENJI. All right then, let's begin again. *(Again, SADAKO runs very fast to the music. Again, GRANDMOTHER makes her magical gesture. SADAKO falls.)* Sadako?

(handwritten in left margin: CONCERN.)

SADAKO. I'm okay. Just a little dizzy, that's all. *(Staccato music begins again very fast, but SADAKO is slowing down.)*

KENJI. Discipline, Sadako! *(She speeds up, we can see that she is in pain but she picks up the pace of the run.)*

SADAKO. I'm trying, Grandmother. I want to win, Grandmother. I want to fly like the wind!

GRANDMOTHER/ACTOR 2. I hear you, Sadako! *(SADAKO moves slowly in a circle, obviously dizzy.)*

(KENJI and GRANDMOTHER become ACTORS 1 and 2. During the following lines, masks on poles will be carried and moved in the air by ACTORS 1 and 2. The masks will be stark white and ghostly. ACTORS 1 and 2 may use many voices and the lines should run into each other to give the impression of many. SADAKO tries to escape the floating faces but they dance around her, bearing down to force her to bed. Recorded music uses a gong sound and heavy beat.)

ACTOR 1. What is the matter with Sadako?

ACTOR 2. What is the matter with Sadako?

ACTOR 1. Why did she fall?

ACTOR 2. Why did she fall?

ACTOR 1. What could be wrong?

ACTOR 2. What could be wrong?

SADAKO. Nothing! I'm just tired, that's all!

ACTOR 1. X-ray her chest.

ACTOR 2. Examine her blood.

ACTOR 1. Put her in a hospital.

ACTORS 1 and 2. Hospital, hospital, hospital...

SADAKO. A hospital? No!

ACTOR 1. Put her to bed.

ACTOR 2. Put her to bed.

SADAKO. But there's nothing wrong with me!

ACTOR 1. Why did she fall?

ACTOR 2. Why did she fall?

ACTOR 1. Take some more tests.

ACTOR 2. Take some more tests.

ACTOR 1. You'll be just fine.

ACTOR 2. Now don't you worry.

ACTOR 1. Don't you worry.

ACTOR 2. Put her to bed.

SADAKO. But I'll miss the race!

ACTOR 1. Now don't you worry.

ACTOR 2. You'll be just fine.

ACTOR 1. Put her to bed.

SADAKO. I want to fly like the wind!

ACTORS 1 and 2 *(holding white masks above their stands)*. Leukemia, leukemia, leukemia, leukemia, leukemia, leukemia...

SADAKO. Leukemia?

(ACTORS 1 and 2 drop masks into holders with a jarring thud. They become MOTHER and FATHER speaking with faces forward as if speaking to a doctor.)

MOTHER. Leukemia? My little girl? But that's impossible! The atom bomb didn't even do so much as scratch her!

FATHER. The atom-bomb sickness? My daughter?

SADAKO. But it can't be true, Mother, can it? *(MOTHER and FATHER rush to her seated on the bench.)* I don't have any scars from the bomb. It didn't touch me. It can't be true, can it, Mother?

FATHER. There now, dear, they just want to do some more tests.

SADAKO. But how can I be sick from the bomb? It killed my grandmother but I wasn't hurt at all.

MOTHER *(very gently)*. Sadako, the radiation doesn't always show up right away.

SADAKO *(terrified)*. I was only two when the bomb fell.

FATHER. It's just a few tests, that's all, sweetheart.

MOTHER. You'll be here a few weeks.

SADAKO. But the race...*(MOTHER and FATHER are fighting back tears.)*

MOTHER. We'll be back everyday to see you. *(Rushes off to hide tears, to music stand.)*

FATHER. Get some rest, sweetheart. *(Kisses her. Exits to music stand.)*

SADAKO. The race...

(ACTOR 1 prepares to become KENJI. Using the instruments to punctuate her lines, ACTOR 2 counts.)

ACTOR 2. Two hundred and thirty-four, two hundred and thirty-five, two hundred and thirty-six, two hundred and thirty-seven...*(The counting fades and SADAKO counts. Again, the primary numbers are spoken together by ACTORS 1 and 2 and SADAKO.)*

SADAKO. Six, seven, eight, nine, ten...

(KENJI enters the scene.)

KENJI. What are you counting?

SADAKO *(sees him, delighted)*. Oh, Kenji, I'm so glad you're here! *(They embrace.)*

KENJI. What's so interesting out there?

SADAKO. I am counting how many trees I can see from my window. This morning I counted the flowers. There were fifty-two. You know, it's only been ten years since the bomb destroyed everything. But look how many trees have grown since then!

KENJI. I have a present for you.

SADAKO. You do?

KENJI. Close your eyes. *(She squinches them very tight, KENJI puts a piece of gold paper on the bed and some scissors.)* Now you can look.

SADAKO *(looking at paper)*. What is it?

KENJI *(laughs)*. I've figured out a way for you to get well. Watch! *(He slowly folds paper into origami crane. Recorded music used earlier in the mimed folding is heard. He holds the crane in the palm of his hand as if it is very precious and holds it out to SADAKO.)*

SADAKO. Kenji, it's beautiful. *(Takes crane.)* But how can this paper crane make me well?

KENJI. Don't you remember that old story about the crane? It's supposed to live for a thousand years. If a sick person folds one thousand paper cranes, the gods will grant her wish and make her healthy again. There's your first one.

SADAKO *(very touched)*. Oh, Kenji, it's beautiful.

KENJI. Make a wish. *(The magical sound of chimes is heard from the music stand. SADAKO holds it out before her, closes her eyes, and her lips move silently. She looks up to KENJI, very moved by his gift.)*

SADAKO. Thank you, Kenji. Thank you.

KENJI. Don't thank me. You have to fold the rest yourself.

SADAKO. I'll start today. *(Looks around.)* But I'll need paper.

KENJI *(putting her on)*. Now where in the world could we get some paper? *(Pretends to think, then pulls some out of his satchel.)* Well, what do you know? Look what I have here. *(Hands it to her.)* This ought to keep you busy.

SADAKO *(takes the paper, smiles at his fun, becomes serious)*. Kenji?

KENJI. Yes?

SADAKO *(trying to be strong)*. Who won the race?

KENJI *(carefully)*. Oh, I don't remember her name. She wasn't very fast. She was a turtle.

SADAKO. But you always said *I* was a turtle.

KENJI. Oh, well, I was only teasing when I said that. You're more like that crane there. You run very fast, Sadako, like a bird. Like the wind.

SADAKO *(almost ready to cry, bolsters herself)*. So if I'm not a turtle, does that mean you're not a frog?

KENJI. What? Me? A frog. Why, that's the silliest thing I ever heard...Croak! Oops! There's that sound again. Croak! Uh-oh. It's starting again, Sadako. Look! Croak! I'm turning all green and warty! Croak! Croak! *(He continues to play the frog until SADAKO is laughing helplessly.)*

(A percussion sound bridges the scene into transition. ALL count together. ACTOR 1 brings bough of paper cranes to SADAKO, moves back to music stand. ACTORS 1 and 2 fade away and become MOTHER and FATHER. SADAKO continues counting. She is holding a very long rope of colorful paper cranes.)

ACTORS 1 and 2 and SADAKO. Four hundred and thirty-two, four hundred and thirty-three, four hundred and thirty-four, four hundred and thirty-five...

SADAKO *(cheerful, counting cranes).* Four hundred and thirty-six, four hundred and thirty-seven, four hundred and thirty-eight!

(She holds them up for MOTHER and FATHER who have just entered.)

SADAKO. See. *(MOTHER and FATHER are very pleased to see her so happy and energetic.)* Kenji taught me! You shouldn't worry about me anymore. Kenji figured out a way for me to get well. Do you remember the story? If a sick person folds a thousand paper cranes then the gods will make her well again. And look. I've already folded four hundred and thirty-eight! *(She holds them up, proud and delighted, full of new vigor.)*

MOTHER. Oh, I'm so glad. I thought you would be sad about not being able to run in the races.

SADAKO *(trying to hide her sudden sadness).* Oh, that. Oh, I don't think about that old race anymore. Silly old race. What good was it? Kenji said I was better than the girl who ran. He said I run like a bird. It's like I'm flying, he said. Folding cranes is much better than any old race. *(MOTHER and FATHER glance at each other.)* It's kind of like a race anyway, don't you think? If I fold them fast enough I won't have to die. *(SADAKO smiles radiantly at her parents. Her MOTHER gasps and grabs SADAKO, pressing her daughter's head against her breast and cries. Pause. MOTHER and FATHER move away, leaving SADAKO alone. She is asleep and speaks with her eyes closed.)* Mother? Mother, where are you? Father? Oh, just you wait, Father. I'll make you so proud of me! I'm going to win. I'm going to win! Oh, but Mother! Father? Where are you now? I don't like it here. It's lonely and I don't feel well. It hurts. It HURTS!!

(ACTORS 1 and 2 become DOCTORS and enter the scene.)

ACTOR 1. What's the matter with Sadako?
ACTOR 2. What's the matter with Sadako?
ACTOR 1. Why did she fall?
ACTOR 2. What could be wrong?
ACTOR 1. Put her to bed.
ACTOR 2. Put her to bed.
SADAKO. No, I don't want to stay in bed!
ACTOR 1. Now don't you worry.
ACTOR 2. You'll be just fine.
SADAKO. But it hurts! And I have such bad dreams.
ACTORS 1 and 2. Put her to bed. Put her to bed. Put her to bed. Put her to bed. *(They repeat as they move away, their voices fading to a whisper.)*
SADAKO. Grandmother? Grandmother? Can you see me? Can you hear me now?

(There is a dramatic percussion sound from ACTOR 1 as ACTOR 2 dons her magnificent GRANDMOTHER mask and enters the scene. (She makes a grand entrance with beautiful recorded music and chimes.)

GRANDMOTHER. I hear you, Sadako.
SADAKO *(slowly opens her eyes, pause, sees GRAND-MOTHER)*. Grandmother! You came back! You returned to earth just like they said.
GRANDMOTHER. Yes, I have returned to help you, Sadako.

SADAKO. Oh, Grandmother, I hurt so much! It's so cold and lonely here. Can I go home now?

GRANDMOTHER *(beckoning)*. I have come to show you something. Come.

SADAKO. Oh, I wish I could go with you, Grandmother.

GRANDMOTHER. I will take you to the mountains and rivers of our ancestors.

SADAKO. Oh, but, Grandmother, how can I go with you? They won't even let me leave my room. They say I have to stay in bed.

GRANDMOTHER. You know a way.

SADAKO. I do?

(GRANDMOTHER stands stoically as ACTOR 1 brings imagined piece of paper downstage as before. He gently smoothes it on the floor before SADAKO, bows and moves upstage again.)

SADAKO. Of course. Yes, now I know.

(SADAKO performs the mimed folding of a giant crane. This is a kind of choreographed dance that was used in the introduction. The "folding" is accompanied by specific music used in each folding sequence. GRAND-MOTHER moves with SADAKO as she folds in a way that suggests she is directing SADAKO. When the folding is complete, GRANDMOTHER and SADAKO look at each other, then slowly move down to lift the crane together. As they stoop to pick up the crane, a dramatic music with gong sound begins. They carry the crane to bench, SADAKO on left side, GRANDMOTHER on right. They place bench/crane C. GRANDMOTHER stands on bench behind her and ACTOR 1 stands on

*floor with back to AUDIENCE behind GRAND-
MOTHER. A whooshing sound is heard as ACTORS con-
tract together to suggest the launching of the bird into
flight. ACTOR 1 uses mylar streamers to "flap" elegantly
as wings. SADAKO is thrilled. ACTOR 1 counts loud
and dramatically, indicating the excitement of the mo-
ment. Loud, beautiful, fast-paced music accompanies
their glorious flight.)*

ACTOR 1. Five hundred and sixty-three, five hundred
and sixty-four, five hundred and sixty-five!

SADAKO *(thrilled)*. Look, Grandmother, it's just like
Kenji said. I fly like the wind! I fly like the wind!

ACTOR 1. Five hundred and seventy-one! Five hundred
and seventy-two! FIVE HUNDRED AND SEVENTY-
THREE!!!

SADAKO. I FLY LIKE THE WIND!! *(ACTOR 1 moves
before SADAKO and GRANDMOTHER, using the mylar streamers to suggest fires on the ground before them.
SADAKO points to streamers.)* Look, Grandmother!

GRANDMOTHER. The Yaizu River.

SADAKO. But it's burning.

GRANDMOTHER. It is All Soul's Day. The day of the
spirits.

SADAKO. There are hundreds of little boats with candles!

GRANDMOTHER. The spirits have visited their loved
ones tonight, just as I have visited you. The candles in
the river are "farewell fires." Soon the spirits will join us.

SADAKO. Join *us?* You mean I'll be able to meet the
spirits?

GRANDMOTHER. Yes.

SADAKO. How wonderful! *(She is very excited, anxiously looking down for a glimpse of the SPIRITS. Pointing.)* There! There! Grandmother, look! *(ACTOR 1 moves around them in a circle holding red masks on poles which seem to "float" around SADAKO and GRAND-MOTHER.)*

GRANDMOTHER. Those are spirits of a thousand, thousand years.

SADAKO *(delighted)*. A thousand, thousand years?

GRANDMOTHER. Yes. They were once young like you, Sadako.

SADAKO. Like me?

GRANDMOTHER. Yes.

SADAKO *(pointing)*. Look! He looks like an *Emperor!* *(ACTOR 1 circles around them, holding a parasol above his head. He moves regally and spins at the sound of gongs which announce his presence. As he moves away, GRANDMOTHER bows to him.)*

GRANDMOTHER. Their valley is deep and their mountains hard to climb. We need not visit there. Our mountain is just ahead.

ACTOR 1 *(using streamers as wings again)*. Five hundred and ninety-three! Five hundred and ninety-four! Five hundred and ninety-five!

GRANDMOTHER *(gesturing to a place before them)*. Here is where we will stop.

(ACTOR 1 slows the wings; they mime landing with a whoosh sound as before. ACTOR 1 gently flutters the streamers down to a halt. The music changes from ex-citement to a quiet, eerie sound of wind instruments. This music will continue through the speeches of the SPIR-ITS. GRANDMOTHER dismounts the crane, gestures to

SADAKO to do the same. SADAKO jumps off the crane, excited with anticipation. ACTOR 1 moves bench. GRANDMOTHER offers SADAKO her arm and leads her around the stage. SADAKO is looking eagerly around. ACTOR 1 puts red mask in holder. He stands behind the waist-high mask among the pastel fans.)

GRANDMOTHER *(gesturing toward mask).* This is the spirit of Mr. Araki. *(ACTOR 1 opens an oriental paper parasol. When he speaks for a SPIRIT he will stand behind that mask with the parasol opened above his head. He does not alter his voice to suggest SPIRIT's voices.)*

ACTOR 1/MR. ARAKI. I was helping to build fire lanes for Hiroshima. The enemy may come soon they said, we must build fire lanes. I was digging with my shovel. I saw the metal grow bright before me. I watched it melt. Everything turned white. Then I was here.

(ACTOR 1 moves parasol in front of his face, closes it as he turns away, leaving the red masks. GRANDMOTHER again offers SADAKO her arm and walks her around the stage as ACTOR 1 places another red mask in its holder. SADAKO is growing confused and a little frightened.)

GRANDMOTHER *(gesturing).* This is the spirit of Mrs. Watanabe.

ACTOR 1/MRS. WATANABE *(opens parasol).* I had just prepared a breakfast for my baby boy. I was bending over his basket to pick him up when I felt a tremendous wind blow me across the room. My baby boy has not joined me here. *(Closes parasol as before, leaving the red mask. Again GRANDMOTHER leads SADAKO on her arm, around and up to third red mask.)*

GRANDMOTHER *(gesturing)*. This is the spirit of Daisuke.

ACTOR 1/DAISUKE. I was seven years old when I came here. I had studied my lessons hard for an examination. I was walking to school. I looked up to see a bird fly. Suddenly the sky was on fire. *(Closes parasol, moves to music stand, leaving three red masks placed among the pastel fans.)*

SADAKO *(horrified, looking at the masks)*. The bomb. They're all talking about the bomb that fell when I was two years old.

GRANDMOTHER. The bomb brought me here, Sadako. *(ACTOR 1 begins to count, continues during this conversation.)*

ACTOR 1. Six hundred and twenty-eight, six hundred and twenty-nine...

SADAKO. Yes, I remember.

ACTOR 1. Six hundred and thirty-one, six hundred and thirty-two...

GRANDMOTHER. The bomb has brought you here, Sadako. You must stay with us.

SADAKO *(realizing what GRANDMOTHER means, pleading)*. But how can that be? I'm twelve years old now. It's been ten years since the bomb fell.

GRANDMOTHER. The bomb continues to fall, Sadako. It is falling even now. *(GRANDMOTHER gestures to ACTOR 1 who pauses in his counting. He brings his head up slowly to look directly at SADAKO. Pause. He resumes his counting.)*

SADAKO *(panicking)*. But my cranes! I've been folding my cranes as fast as I can!

ACTOR 1. Six hundred and thirty-nine...

SADAKO *(pleading)*. I haven't folded a thousand yet!

GRANDMOTHER *(assuring)*. You will have a thousand. You'll see. It is better to leave them for others to finish.

SADAKO. Someone will finish them for me? But then how can the cranes grant my wish?

GRANDMOTHER *(lovingly)*. What did you wish for, Sadako? *(ACTOR 1 stops counting but continues percussion rhythm during the following line.)*

SADAKO. To make you live. To make me better. I wished that there will never ever be a bomb like that again. *(Silence. ACTOR 1 moves dramatically from music stand carrying closed parasol before him as if it is something very precious. He ceremoniously gives it to GRANDMOTHER, bows and returns to his place behind the music stand. GRANDMOTHER moves to SADAKO, holds parasol out to her, nods to encourage her. SADAKO takes the parasol, GRANDMOTHER moves away. ACTOR 1 begins rhythm again. They count together.*

ACTOR 1 and GRANDMOTHER. Six hundred and forty-one, six hundred and forty-two, six hundred and forty-three...

SADAKO *(solemn)*. Six hundred and forty-four. *(There is the sound of the bomb as she opens the parasol above her head, then brings it down in front of her, like a shield, hiding her face. GRANDMOTHER and ACTOR 1 bow their heads. The bomb sound continues as SADAKO moves to take her place in the fans with the other red masks. Lifts parasol.)* I was two years old and my mother held me in her arms. She sang a song to me. It was a quiet summer morning. Inside our small house my grandmother was preparing tea. Suddenly there was a tremendous flash of light that cut across the sky. *(She moves her parasol to cover her face as before.)*

(The bomb sound is quieter this time and slowly fades away. ACTOR 1 becomes KENJI. KENJI enters the scene calling to SADAKO. He uses the bill of his hat as before to make a large mouth for his comical frog. The bill covers his eyes.

KENJI *(playful)*. Sadako! Oh, Sadako...How's the lazy little turtle this morning? You know, I think you're right. I'm becoming more of a frog every day. Why just this morning I found two warts on my foot. Now what do you make of that? Croak! See, there's that sound again. *(Hopping to her bed.)* You want to see my warts? *(He puts his cap back to see her, laughing. He is stopped when he sees that she is not there.)* Sadako? *(Looks around.)* Sadako? *(He sees rope of cranes, holds it, then sits on the bench. He solemnly removes his hat and bows his head.)*

(From her place at the music stand, ACTOR 2 narrates.)

ACTOR 2. Sadako Sasaki died on October 25, 1955. Her friends and classmates folded three hundred and fifty-six cranes to make a thousand. *(KENJI stands, moves U, mimes getting the large piece of paper as before. He gracefully places it downstage. The folding music begins, KENJI mimes folding movements of giant crane as SADAKO has done. ACTOR 2 begins recorded folding music and moves from the stand to DL.)* Sadako's friends began to dream of building a monument to her and all the children who were killed by the atom bomb. In 1958, the statue was unveiled in the Hiroshima Peace Park. There is Sadako standing on top of a granite mountain. She is holding a golden crane in outstretched arms.

KENJI *(as he folds)*. Nine hundred and ninety-seven...

ACTOR 2. Now every year, children from all over Japan visit her memorial...

KENJI. Nine hundred and ninety-eight...

ACTOR 2. And bring thousands of paper cranes to her monument.

KENJI. Nine hundred and ninety-nine...

ACTOR 2. Their wish is engraved on the base of the statue: *(KENJI begins to stand, slowly miming the lifting of the giant crane. He uses both hands as SADAKO did in the beginning. It is very light.)*

"This is our cry,

This is our prayer,

Peace in the World."

KENJI. One thousand. *(He launches it in the air and blows after it as SADAKO has done before. His outstretched arms follow the path of the bird's flight, turning to a point, indicating the flight across the sky. ACTOR 2 watches the bird with KENJI. From her position U, SADAKO moves her parasol from its shield-like position, holding it above her head. She watches the flight of the bird with KENJI and ACTOR 2. She points up.)*

SADAKO *(joyous)*. Look, Grandmother! You were right! *(ALL freeze.)*

END

CORRECT PRONUNCIATION
OF JAPANESE NAMES

*HIROSHIMA
He-ro-*she*-mah or He-ro-she-*mah*
the "r" is slightly trilled.

*ARAKI
A-rah-*kee*
the "r" is slightly trilled.

*WATANABE
Wah-tah-nah-*bay*

*DAISUKE
Di-soo-*kay*
the "d" is almost make like a "th".

*SADAKO
Sah-dah-ko
the "d" is almost made like a "th".

THE SQUARE PRELIMINARY FOLD

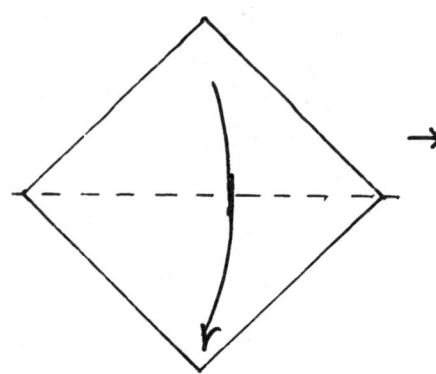

Start with un colored side up
and make a diagonal fold.

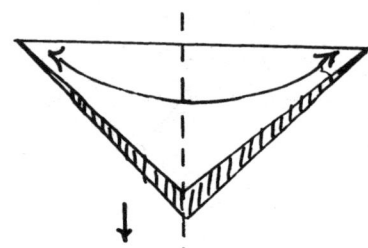

2. Make a preliminary vertical
crease, using a second diagonal
fold.

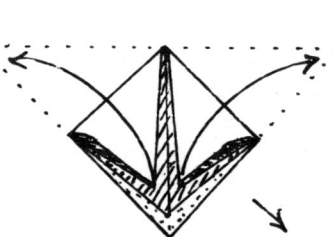

Unfold both folds.

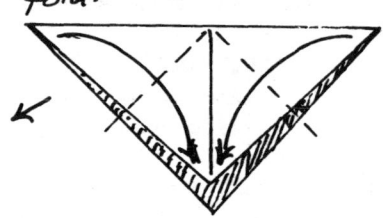

3. Fold both upper right and upper
left edges along center line.

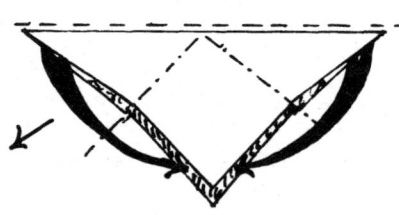

5. Inside-reverse-fold each side,
following preliminary creases.
(It is necessary to open the figure
partially and to reverse the creases
on top to tuck corners inside the flap.)

Valley Fold   — — — — —

Mountain Fold   — · — · — · —

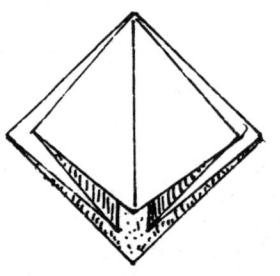

The square preliminary fold.

THE BIRD BASE

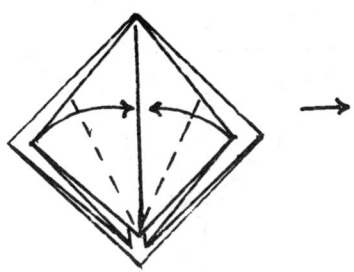

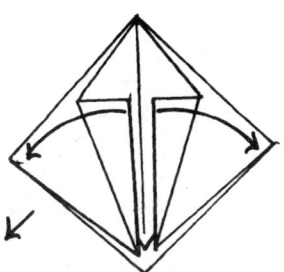

1. Start with a square preliminary fold. Fold lower sides of right and left flaps to center lines.

2. Unfold both right and left flaps.

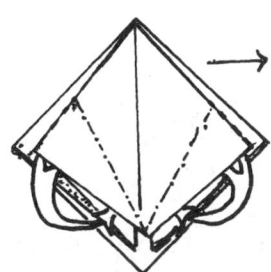

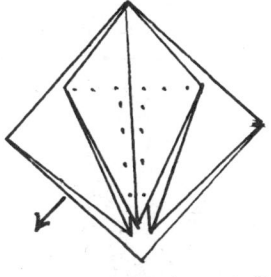

3. Use an inside reverse fold to tuck corners of right and left flaps inside. (It is necessary to reverse the creases on top and lift up the top sheet to slip in the side corner.)

4. Repeat steps 1-3 on reverse side.

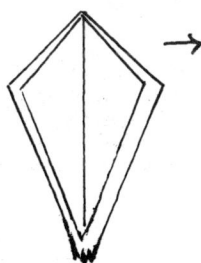

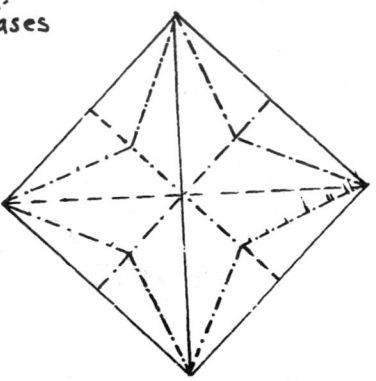

5. The bird base.

6. Creases of the bird base.

THE SITTING CRANE
-Traditional Folding-

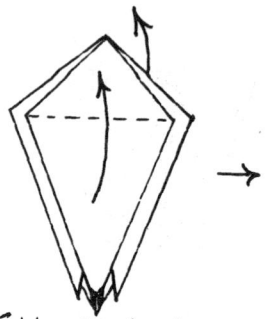

1. Fold up the front and rear flaps of the bird base.

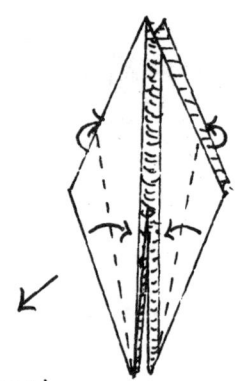

2. Fold in lower sides to center line. Repeat behind.

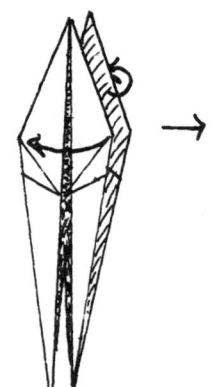

3. Book-fold the figure front and back.

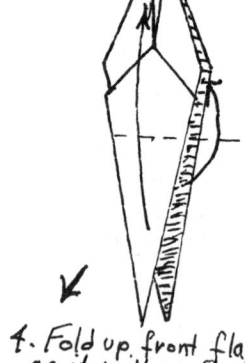

4. Fold up front flap as far as it will go. Repeat behind. (One becomes the neck, the other, the tail.)

5. Book-fold the front and back exposing the wider wings.

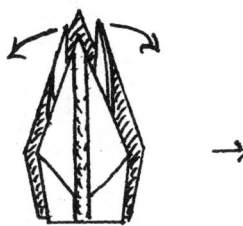

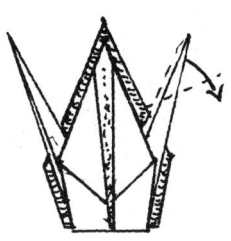

6. Move neck and tail flush with edges of body.

7. Inside-reverse-fold one third of neck to form a head.

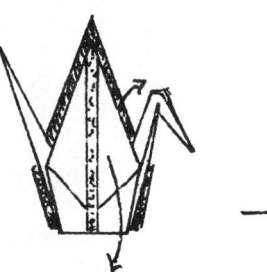

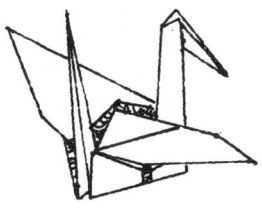

8. Pull wings down into a horizontal position.

9. The sitting crane.

WHAT PEOPLE ARE SAYING about *A Thousand Cranes*...

"It is a wonderful script that gives the actors and director complete artistic choice. There were very few dry eyes in the house at the end of this performance."
Stephanie Brotherton,
Marion C. Early High School,
Morrisville, Mo.

"*A Thousand Cranes* is a story about a victim of Hiroshima. It is a timely story since it deals with the aftermath of war. And although written by a Westerner shows much sensitivity for the Japanese culture."
Paulette Brockington,
Sterling Heights High School,
Sterling Heights, Mich.

"*Very beautiful and imaginative.*"
Trudianne Thom,
Waterford Union High School,
Waterford, Wis.

"This is a beautiful story and a very good one to use for UIL one-act play competition."
Ava Johnson,
Molina High School,
Dallas, Texas

DIRECTOR'S NOTES

Maddy opening statement needs to be more powerful.

* every one looking deadpan out.
* Flash of light Fade out of move over song.
* Slow Fall.
* messy into Plane section. umbrella set wrong.
* Out of plane too masks Jolt.

Maddy more banter / callum up you gone.
Strong Positions from chorces.
callum you must be Joly.
Stan strong and bold about

Actions -

Stan its not a Primary School Play

Maddy move Panicard in your voice about Finding gran /when your saying number theres no intention
· Callam theres no story there no relationship.

· look At whats a matter with Salhota bit

· Why the crouched beat Parents
o Relationship callum · Feel the Music · react they show it.

DIRECTOR'S NOTES

○ Stop being so dramatic with
New could we Find [?]

• Motive and Intentions Parents
Dada

○ Sathana Story telling moments.
maddly feelings and emotion.

○ More enjoyment in Sunday No

DIRECTOR'S NOTES

DIRECTOR'S NOTES

DIRECTOR'S NOTES